Three Feet from Seven Figures:
One-on-One Engagement Techniques
to Qualify More Leads at Trade Shows

by David Spark

Paperback ISBN: 978-0-9968602-0-8

David Spark (@dspark) is the founder and president of
Spark Media Solutions, a brand journalism firm based in
the San Francisco Bay Area.

Spark blogs at Spark Minute and podcasts weekly on the Tear Down Show.

For more information about trade show training, or to book
David Spark for interviews and speaking engagements,
please contact info@sparkmediasolutions.com.

Illustrations by Christina Taylor Brown (@stinabmarie).

Cover design and book layout by Joy Powers (@joypowers).

2018 printing

www.ThreeFeetBook.com

THREE FEET

from

SEVEN FIGURES

One-on-One Engagement Techniques
to Qualify More Leads at Trade Shows

by DAVID SPARK

At a trade show, your booth is like a stage. Anything you do in that booth is presented to an ever passing audience. It's grueling because this show goes on continuously with no intermissions for eight to ten hours each day. If a booth staffer gets bored and stares at their phone or turns their back to the people walking by, it reflects poorly on that staffer, the booth, and the company. Even with the spectacular booth design, giveaways, and videos playing, attendees see the booth staffers and their behavior first.

You may be attracted by a cool booth design, but you don't walk up to it and have a conversation.

In preparing for this book, I wanted to prove that unapproachable booth behavior was systemic. At a tech industry trade show, I hired a photographer to take pictures of any bad behavior she saw. I gave her the whole day, but in just two hours she came back with dozens of photos of people staring at their computer, browsing their phone, or chatting with coworkers.

To the people walking by, all of these photos could have been captioned "Don't bother me," "I'm not professional," or "I don't want to be here."

No one sees how bad this is until they're at the show. Or, and this is more often the case, they never see it as bad behavior because they're not the ones watching it. They think, "This is what I normally do every day. I work on my computer, check my phone, and talk to my coworkers." A trade show is not your normal work day. Unlike at the office, at a trade show you're on display all day.

In preparing for a trade show, we focus only on physical logistics, such as booth design, shipping equipment, giveaways, messaging, video production, booking hotels, and flying staffers to the show.

What's left behind in all that planning are preparing the people on what to expect at the show, how to behave, and how to identify and qualify the best possible leads.

HOW ARE YOU GOING TO GET THE RIGHT PEOPLE TO STOP, COME INTO THE BOOTH, AND ENGAGE WITH YOU?

Engagement often begins with an opening line. But it's more than that — you also need to learn how to engage, qualify, create follow-up points, end the conversation, and then start it all over again very quickly. You're playing a fast-paced "round robin" game of business speed dating with complete strangers in an unreal environment.

It's easy to play the game poorly, and think you're doing well. Just because you stood in your booth all day and talked to tons of people, doesn't necessarily mean you achieved your objectives.

Working at a trade show is work. It's really hard work. To some degree it's a performance, yet you want to play the part of yourself. Still, we must call it a "performance" because you're required to be consistently "on" more than you would be on any other given day and in any other environment.

A trade show floor is like a corporate version of "Burning Man." Thousands of people come together to a specific location to create this small intense city that's only open for a few days for a certain number of hours. After that brief period of time ends, the city is torn down and it all disappears. Everyone will come back again and meet next year.

You are so close to so much.

Think about your five best customers. How long have they been customers? How much revenue have they brought into your company? If you're a B2B business, the answer is probably in the seven figures.

Now look at the people circling your trade show booth. As you watch them passing by, imagine them with that multi-million dollar lifetime value figure floating over their head.

That person with the dollar figure over their head may not be the person who ultimately signs the deal. But that person may connect you to a key person and that person may influence another person's decision, and so on, and so on.

Now look at your employees. Are they talking to who could be million dollar customers? Wouldn't they be behaving a lot differently if they knew they were "three feet from seven figures?"

Behavior at a trade show should be about non-stop engagement. Conversely, employees told to staff the booth can't always handle this "always on" pressure and they shut down because they don't know how to behave in the unreal environment of a trade show floor.

The purpose of this book is to bring back that focus so that you don't lose out on that opportunity that keeps walking by you... only three feet away.

Too much reliance on everything but the people.

We're comfortable coordinating *things*. If we get all the elements of a booth coordinated correctly, then we've done our job and we'll have a successful show. That's what we've fooled ourselves into believing.

At one point your customers were not customers. How did they become customers? Was it through a series of conversations with key people in your company, or did they happen to get a company-branded T-shirt and then call you up and place an order?

Your most talented and outgoing employees are your greatest asset, yet the time and money spent at trade shows and conferences is rarely focused on the people and their ability to engage. It's spent on everything else but that.

The reality is trade show production avoids the most important issue, which is preparing people for how they'll behave when they're actually working in the booth.

Even if you don't want to talk about and train booth behavior, you absolutely have to because the reality is...

...Most people don't reach out.

Sadly, the majority of people I see managing a booth are not proactive. They're not the first to reach out and engage with complete strangers. This can be for a variety of factors:

- They believe their job is to just be a passive body in the booth and just answer any questions people may have.

- They don't have the social constitution to make introductions with complete strangers.

- They can't deal with or may feel they're too senior for any type of rejection.

- They would be more proactive, but they simply don't know what they should do.

- They would be more proactive, but they haven't practiced enough to be comfortable doing it at a live event.

- They feel more comfortable talking with their coworkers than trying to meet a complete stranger.

- They simply don't understand how critical it is to engage with attendees.

It's a situation of being uncomfortable and not prepared for a trade show, an environment that is admittedly not normal.

It doesn't need to be that way if you...

...Learn how to play the *last three feet.*

The purpose of this book is to make you a "last three feet" winner, and to demonstrate how your staff can close that last three-foot gap between themselves and what could be a seven-figure customer. Assuming your goal extends beyond just being seen, trade show success is rarely determined by who has the coolest booth. Nor is it determined by who collected the most business cards.

The true winners have <u>the most positive qualified engagements</u>.

To be able to have <u>*the most positive qualified engagements*</u>, you need to be able to do the following:

Step 1: BREAK THE ICE
Find a point to begin an engagement.

Step 2: CREATE A RAPPORT
Find a *business* reason to keep engaging.

Step 3: QUALIFY THE PERSON QUICKLY
Is this person right for your business?

Step 4: TELL YOUR STORY
Qualified or not, everyone should know your story and be able to retell it.

Step 5: COLLECT CONVERSATIONAL INFORMATION
Record information about your one-on-one engagement, not just a badge scan.

Step 6: END THE CONVERSATION
End most engagements, qualified or not, quickly and positively so that you're free to engage with others.

Step 7: REPEAT

The ability to successfully pull off all these steps can't be found in a great booth design or glitzy video. The look and activities at the booth are critical for attracting crowds. Alone they can't create the engagement. Only you and your staff can create a conference's most sought-after asset: relationships.

When you leave a conference, what's the most memorable aspect? Is it the cool booth you went to, or the great conversations you had? And what causes you to follow up with someone? Is it because of a great video you saw or an amazing giveaway? Or is it because you made a true connection and discussed a problem or a possible opportunity?

What follows is some advice on how to make that initial connection and how to qualify the value of that relationship. The information is culled from experts in trade show presentation and production, and from my own experience working in corporate entertainment and production.

Read the following advice, practice it, adhere to it, and I guarantee your next experience working a trade show will be more successful than the last one.

Before we begin...

...Fully understand your hourly costs on the trade show floor.

Open up a spreadsheet and add up all the money you're going to be spending before and at the trade show. Include the following costs in your spreadsheet:

- Booth sponsorship

- Design and production of signage

- Rental or purchase of booth equipment

- Hiring of staff (often union members) to set up the booth

- Public relations to drum up industry press

- Giveaways, including business card "raffle" drawings and drinks or meals with leads

- Produced demos and videos

- Employees' time (often months) before the event to produce the booth

- Mini-events and cocktails

- Air travel for all employees

- Cab fare and rental cars for all employees

- Hotels for all employees

- Meals and other incidentals for all employees

- Salary of employees while at the event

- Lost value/opportunity cost of employees not back at the office doing their job

Add up *all* those costs and then divide it by the number of hours the trade show floor will be open. If it's a two-day event and the floor will be open for a total of 16 hours, divide all your costs by 16. See a really big number? That's your hourly cost to be at the trade show.

Matt Hill, President of The Hill Group, said that **ONE CUSTOMER CALCULATED THAT IT WAS COSTING HIM $35,000 AN HOUR TO BE AT THE TRADE SHOW**. It's very possible you're dropping that kind of money, or perhaps it's costing you a fraction of that. Regardless, it's still too much unless you know how to get a decent return on your investment.

A trade show is an enormous gamble. How do you stack the odds against everyone else so you're the winner?

While Disney refers to their employees as "cast members"...

...Your trade show work should be viewed as a complete performance.

Many people think that if they just go through the mechanics of standing in the booth, give demos to people who come up to them, and then hand out giveaways, they've done enough. It's not. A trade show experience is a complete performance that requires choreography among all the people in the booth, not just the person you hired to give presentations. And it's not only what you say in the booth that's important, it's what you don't say, because...

...Non-verbal communications speak loudest.

Your behavior in the booth is sending a louder message to all the people walking by your booth than anything being displayed in your booth, including the signage. If you're talking to your coworkers, eating, drinking, looking at your phone, or working on your computer, what kind of message do you think that sends to the people walking by your booth? Do you think anyone wants to talk to you? All of that behavior is being watched by people as they're walking by your booth, and none of it is inviting. Because of the non-verbal message you're sending, they're rejecting you before they even talk to you. In such a case you're getting hundreds if not thousands of rejections, with no possibility of a positive engagement.

Being rejected through the subtext of your actions will start you in a hole, and you don't need to add more complexity because working a trade show introduces a new pressure-inducing variable...

...You're always fighting time.

Once you understand your hourly costs on the trade show floor, and what limited time you have to make an impact, then you'll understand how important it is that your staff works every minute to their utmost potential. When you're on the floor, opportunities are constantly ticking away. You're constantly fighting time. Before you arrive at the show, your staff must be fully prepared and motivated to work hard and comfortably engage with complete strangers.

Being able to work those last three feet, between you and the people at the show, is the most critical aspect for your business' success.

How you do that depends on knowing the answer to...

...What are your goals?

What do you want to get out of the show?

- Do you want leads? What kind of leads do you want? What would qualify a person as being a "good lead"?

- Do you want to get press? Do you want people to blog about you? Are you looking for social media buzz? Do you want to create your own press and write blog posts or shoot videos at the show?

- Do you want to be seen as an industry leader?

- Do you want to sell product from the show floor?

When you get mired in all the details of a trade show booth's production, coordination, and travel arrangements, it's really easy to miss the most important aspect: Why are we there?

So before we get into the details of approaching attendees at a trade show, ask yourself the following:

- What is our overarching goal for the show? Are there additional subgoals?

- Have we stated our goals? Can all our employees state them as well?

- Have we defined what a successful outcome would look like? How would we measure it?

If your agenda is clear, then your audience will know how and why they should work with you or buy your product. Knowing your agenda is half the battle. The other half is to...

...Know the attendees' agendas.

Your objective at a trade show is to make a connection between your objectives and the attendees' objectives. Do you know what their goals are? Do you really? Or do you just think you know? Chances are you don't really know. The best way to find out is simply to ask.

Try inviting a small group (20 at most) of potential customers, industry analysts and influencers, and journalists out to dinner. Be very clear what the objective is for the get-together. In the invite say that you're just trying to learn what people's interests and objectives are for the upcoming trade show. Don't hide this information from them. Nobody likes to be blindsided by a sales pitch they weren't ready to hear.

Take that information and see how well it meshes with your objectives. Where can you find synergies? Remember, people walking the hall will first and foremost be thinking about themselves and their own agendas. You have to come to them first. Matt Hill advises you to ask yourself: "If you were that person, what is the experience you would like to have?"

If your business is not yet known in the industry, you'll have to introduce yourself. If you are known, everyone is going to have a preconceived notion of who you are so...

...Defend your turf.

Every industry has a big trade show and you have to be there. Not just to get new business, but to protect your existing business. It's the one time you'll see the highest concentration of your audience, specifically the buyers and influencers of your product, in one place.

Many companies sponsor conferences to make new product announcements. Even if you don't have anything new to announce, you need to be at the conference to simply protect the business you already have. When you don't have a presence at a conference, it gives your competition license and provocation to define your situation for you. Count on it being negative.

When an attendee says, "I'm surprised I don't see Company XYZ at the show this year," the competition or even influencers who may not know better will say, "Well, they've been having some problems."

You can't be everywhere, but you need to be at your industry's most important conferences.

A lot of people are a little timid about trade shows. It's understandable. Meeting on a trade show floor is completely unique and unlike any other experience because...

...It's awkward. Accept it.

There's absolutely nothing natural about a trade show environment. It's a mini, temporary, fluorescent-lit city where extremely attractive women are *eager* to talk to everyone. Unlike the real world, a successful engagement on a trade show floor can be determined just by a look or a single opening line. Multiple relationships can be formed in minutes. Salespeople who make their living talking to people and negotiating are often completely unprepared with how to engage in the unreal world of a trade show floor.

Unless you live in a mall, no one is ever prepared for a trade show engagement. Even people who are used to manning a booth, and are very personable, can freeze up in the trade show environment.

That "freezing up" doesn't necessarily manifest itself in being tongue-tied, but rather in retreating to a secure environment, such as huddling with your colleagues. Recognize when this is happening and...

...Break up the booth huddle.

There's nothing less inviting than a bunch of people wearing the same colored shirts, huddled around and talking to each other. While the participants don't realize it, it's pathetic to observers.

"The sales guys all talk to each other because of *fear*," said Mark Norby, EVP of Live Marketing. "It's really hard to proactively reach out and engage with people at a trade show. There's fear of interrupting people and not being accepted."

If you find yourself all of a sudden in a booth huddle, be aware of how others walking by see you. It's uninviting. No one wants to meet you.

Therefore it's your job to tell your fellow huddlers "OK guys, time to break it up" and...

...Treat your booth like your home.

"When someone enters your home, what would you do?" asked Matt Hill. "You wouldn't wait for them to come to you." You would go to them. You'd walk up and be the first to initiate the greeting.

It's not just what you say, it's how you position yourself as you're saying it so...

...Angle people into your booth.

It's natural and comfortable for us to stand square on the edge of our booth as we're talking with people. But to the person you're talking with, you've now become an impediment to actually getting into the booth. To solve this problem, just shift your body so you're angling yourself into the booth, kind of like an open door.

Maintain this "never straight-on approach" and...

BOOTH
Sweet
BOOTH

...Approach people diagonally.

When you walk up to people, approach them at an angle. It's less confrontational and friendlier.

To get them to walk through your door, you'll want to...

...Add comforts of the home to your booth.

Decorate your booth to be inviting just like you would your own home. People feel more comfortable and welcome when they see recognizable home elements such as plants, lamps, couches, coffee tables, beverages, and mints. If you do offer drinks, gain quick acceptance with the opening line, "Can I get you a drink?"

Keep your booth looking presentable. At a trade show, company is constantly coming over and they have no problem leaving garbage all over our home so...

...Always be cleaning up.

Whether you offer food or drinks in your booth or not, other booths are. Garbage will often be left in your booth and it will turn the positive image of a booth costing six figures to zero in an instant.

Unless you hired a catering company to work your booth, no one ever has the solo job of cleaning up. Even if you're the CEO of a billion dollar company, pick up the garbage and throw it out. Don't call someone over to clean it up. Cleaning up is everyone's responsibility.

When you set up the booth, make sure to also include a garbage can if it's not already offered by the venue. Among all the other booth elements, it is a sorely needed and often missed element.

While it's important to keep your booth presentable to everyone, you don't necessarily want everyone in your booth. You simply don't have the time to talk to everyone. You only have time to talk to relevant people. Always be asking yourself...

...Why am I stopping this person?

You could be friendly to everyone, but what is the goal of your presence at the trade show? Are you presenting a new product, are you trying to establish your place in the industry, or are you trying to find people who have a specific issue at their company?

Since time and attention are very precious commodities on a trade show floor, have a very clear objective of what you're trying to achieve, and how you're going to get there with your attendees. They're walking around the floor in a free-floating state. They're not grounded. It's your job to...

...Give attendees a reason to stop.

You shouldn't waste attendees' time or your own time. As you have an agenda, they do too.

You have to be able to say to yourself, "I'm stopping this person for their own good because I can help them," said Mark Norby. If you have the right attitude you're not intruding someone by stopping them, you're doing them a *favor*. That's a really important distinction and important mindset to maintain.

In order to determine who you'll help...

...Look for an opportunity to engage.

There are lots of subtle things you can watch for as engagement points. The most common is when someone stops in front of your booth and drops their eyes, searching for someone or something. Use that as a cue to intercept.

There are other positive clues such as making eye contact with you, smiling, laughing, or otherwise looking like they're generally in a good mood. Ride that positive attitude with an introduction.

While you want to be seen as helpful, please...

...Don't ever ask, "Can I help you?"

This is a horrible opening line. The answer is usually "No" or "Where's the bathroom?" In either case, your conversation is over. It's a wasted engagement that began and ended in a moment. Even if they do ask where the bathroom is, they're not going to want to sit around and chat with you. They have to go.

When you ask "Can I help you?" — you come off as a concierge for the hotel or convention center. That's not your job. You're an industry professional that has something of value to share.

While attendees are often roaming the floor in that free-floating state, they do have an overall agenda. They're there to see something new, learn the latest trends, or meet up with some industry colleagues. After that, and luckily for you, the average attendee's agenda is poorly formed. You can use that lack of "what I'm doing here" clarity to your advantage to stop them, engage in conversation, and dig deeper to find out why they're there so...

...Begin by asking an open-ended question.

One of the most common open-ended questions heard anywhere is "How are you?" But that question is so generic and overused that it has lost all its power to show any true empathy. Anyone who asks "How are you?" on a trade show floor really doesn't care about you at all, nor have they put up much effort into knowing about you. They're just looking for an excuse to get you to stop. It's really no different than when a homeless person stops you to ask what time it is. They don't care. They're just looking for an excuse to get you to engage with them so they can eventually ask "Spare some change?"

Ask a question that engages the person in a true, honest conversation where it's obvious you do actually care about their answer.

My favorite open-ended question is "See anything cool at the show?" This is a perfect question, as it benefits both parties involved even if there isn't a connection. The person trapped in the booth gets to find out what's on the floor while simultaneously learning about the interests of the stopped attendee. The booth staffer can use that information to mesh their two agendas. In return, the person stopped gets an opportunity to share what he or she has learned, bouncing it off an interested party.

Even if you don't think this person will be a qualified lead, you just learned something about the event, the players, and the competition.

While asking "See anything cool on the show?" is a great way to break the ice, it's best to...

...Prepare a few opening lines.

Even if you have the world's greatest opening line, you'll get bored with it quickly and you'll look like a broken record to all the people around you. That's why you should prepare a few opening lines.

When coming up with an opening line, try to address people's innate self-centeredness by asking a question that would concern them. Prepare a few opening lines. You can think of some of your own, but we invite you to be like comedian Milton Berle and steal some great opening lines, such as:

- Are you in a *such and such* situation?

- What solutions are you looking for today?

- What brings you to the trade show today?

- What's the best conversation you've had today?

Consider a little humor with opening lines such as:

- I'm stopping seemingly intelligent people.

- Is this show really that boring?

- I'm looking for suckers, I mean volunteers, to rope into this fun game.

If you want to improve the success of your opening line...

...Acknowledge what's happening that moment.

At a trade show people are more in the moment than constantly "on point." While they came to the conference to find a solution, that's not always top of mind. They may be thinking about how cold it is, how they're aching in their high heels, or how they have a meeting in 30 minutes.

Also, there's lots of stuff going on at the conference that is more pressing than a demo in your booth. Be aware of the other events going on at the conference. If you know people will be rushing to a keynote at the end of the day, maybe that's not a good time to push attendees. Not everything is visible, but there's still plenty to work off of and you can use it to your advantage.

For example, if you see a woman wearing shoes just like yours you could point it out and say "We're wearing the same shoes. You obviously have great taste." Or you could just offer up a compliment with something that's unique to them: "I love your red coat." If you can't identify anything personal on them, ask for their opinion: "What do you think of my blue wig?"

Another option is to acknowledge a big announcement at the trade show.

"Did you hear what _____ said on stage?"

An opening line is the first step, but to have a conversation you'll need to...

...Have three stories in the can.

Companies focus so much on "messaging," and sadly the only people who remember the company messages are the marketing department. We don't retell messages, we retell stories. Have at least three stories prepared that address some of the attendees' key issues. See if you can steer the conversation naturally to those stories. If not, see the previous advice and acknowledge what's happening in the moment.

Being prepared with a few stories will make you much more confident. But even with all the preparation and the great opening lines, you have to...

...Be okay with hearing "No."

One of the many reasons employees don't reach out to complete strangers is they're afraid of rejection. The reality is rejection on a trade show floor is extraordinarily common and frequent.

Not only should you not fear rejection, expect to get lots of it. If 50 people rejected you in person in one day in a non-trade-show environment, it would be monumentally depressing. Given the accelerated and compressed nature of a trade show environment, 50 or more people rejecting you in one day is completely normal, and there's no malice involved or anything to internalize.

If you are on a trade show floor and were engaging with enough people to garner as many as 50 rejections, that means you're probably getting lots more positive engagements. And that means you're doing an amazing job. Rejection on a trade show floor means you're hustling. To echo a very common meme: If you're not getting rejected half the time, you're not trying hard enough.

All of these techniques work well, but there's still one more trick that will *always* get people to stop for a moment and engage with you...

...Read their name off the show badges.

The show badges have the person's name and company printed right on them. Look at the badge and say the person's first name. When people hear their name at a trade show, they likely don't immediately assume it's someone reading off their badge. They think someone they know is calling out to them.

It *always* causes people to stop.

Dropping the first name is an easy opener, yet so few people actually take advantage of reading the name badge. Be a trailblazer in friendly introductions. Say the person's name.

To actually have something to talk about, mention their company name as well. If you actually know the company, you can make a comment such as "Hi Debbie, you're from Sony? I have one of your video cameras and I love it." If she says, "Well, I don't work in that division," you can simply follow up and ask what division she works in.

If you don't know the company at all, you could still incorporate the company name in a silly way: "Edward, you're at Oracle? My uncle is the mayor of Oracle."

Acknowledging people by name and company is a good way to get a foot in the door. To get them to keep listening and like you...

...Endow attendees with positive branding.

People like to be complimented beyond their physical appearance. They want to be appreciated for their actual work or for what you want them to be in your story. When you engage, you need a story and you need them to play the starring roles. You could be talking about a situation at their company for which only Edward, the rock star at Oracle, could handle. Halfway through your story, you could stop saying his name and only refer to him as a "rock star" at his job (e.g., "Steve's a rock star engineer.")

You can also make the designation more specific to your story, for example, by calling your target a "smart buyer" or "top manager." Keep your conversation very positive and unless they're by nature cynical, they won't dismiss you because that would be a rejection of the positive image you're bestowing upon them.

As you can imagine, this can get corny and cheesy if you don't do it correctly. Unless you're an amazing actor, don't endow anyone with a title that makes you feel uncomfortable. Just be positive and honest about their role, and feel free to embellish. People gravitate towards people who compliment them. One other way to get people on your side quickly is to...

...Ask questions for which there's a "yes" sequence.

This is a very old sales technique. Questions such as "Nice weather we're having" and "Crowded show, isn't it?" are each designed to get a simple "yes." With each level of agreement the target gets more and more invested in the discussion.

A "yes" is a low level of engagement. You can get people to increase their level of engagement by asking them to watch something, or even hold something for you. If you create a demonstration where attendees have to participate, they truly become invested.

This "yes" sequencing all stays in line with the number one rule...

...Always stay positive.

No matter how good a conference is, people will find something that irritates them. They'll complain about the companies, the booth, the food, the keynote speaker, or the panel discussions.

Your job is to avoid all of that. Always speak well of the conference, competition, and customers. Even if you're 100 percent in the right about something negative, don't say it because the mere act of saying something negative reflects negatively on you, the speaker.

If the person you're speaking with brings up the competition, you can still be positive without mentioning their product. For example, say "They've got a great booth" or "They throw great parties."

As tired as you may be, you still want to emote posititively. Talk about how something is "fantastic" or "game changing." If you watched any of Steve Jobs' presentations, you'll see he did this a lot. But don't do it just to fill up space. Only say something is "game changing" if you can immediately back it up. People often throw up their BS detectors if they hear these buzzwords with no evidence, demonstration, or explanation.

Be wary of saying "but," as it implies negativity. Affirm what's happening in the moment and offer something that agrees with it. For example, instead of saying "I see you're in a rush, but don't you want to hear about our party?" say "I see you're in a rush now, so I'm going to give you this invite so you can relax at our party tonight."

The theatrical practice of improvisation (AKA "improv") is built on the "Yes, and..." principle which states that no matter what the person says or does, affirm it and offer more.

"Yes, and..." also keeps driving the conversation forward, just like when you...

...Ask lots of questions.

In the U.S. asking questions is one of the top rules of dating (I hear Europeans hate it). If you're in the right cultural environment, it should also be on the top of your queue as you're courting people at trade shows. Ask people what their role is, what they're looking for, if they're looking to solve certain problems, and most importantly ask if they're responsible for purchasing. Make sure you actually listen to their answers and respond to what they're saying. Don't just rattle off a list of your prepared questions.

If you want the person to feel that you really care what they're saying...

...Ask for their opinion.

Simply ask "May I get your opinion on something?" It's a great opener, suggested trainer, comic, and magician Robert Strong.

Other questions you ask can be serious: "What do you think about the state of security?" Or they could be silly: "Do these bunny ears make me look taller?"

While it's important to know what to say, it's also important to know *when* to say it so...

...Find the sweet spot to start the conversation.

In most cases, you'll need to walk up to someone to begin the engagement. Timing as you approach is critical. You'll want to ask your question/opening line just as the two of you meet. If you begin your approach too early, they'll ignore you. If you start too late, they'll be past you.

Even if you get it perfectly right, it doesn't mean they'll engage with you so...

...Follow up even if you're rejected.

While it's important to have an opening line, it's more important to have a follow-up line, because you want the experience to be positive for *them* even if they reject *you*.

Robert Strong has a great technique for this. If people are walking by really fast, he'll ask "Would you like to see the world's fastest card trick?" If they respond "Yes," then he shows them the fast card trick that hooks them in, allowing him to show more. If they say "No," then he responds with "Would you like to see it again?" This usually gets a laugh and makes people circle back around. The second line can be as simple as "Feel free to come back later. We have free giveaways and a guest speaker at 3pm." That way, you turn their rejection into a future opportunity for them.

Sometimes there will be no opportunity to come back later. In those cases...

...Create urgency and scarcity.

You'll see this technique used when a booth is about to show a presentation or have a drawing for a prize. It works when you need to amass a lot of people in your booth very quickly. Simply say "Our drawing is starting in 30 seconds" or "Our presentation is about to begin in one minute. Hurry up."

Even better, post a digital clock with a very visible countdown so people can see that urgency. If they don't believe you, they'll see the clock and then they'll really know the drawing is going to start in 30 seconds.

Chances are you came to the event with 10,000 giveaways. Even if there are 8,000 left, let everyone know these are the last giveaways left. Because your supply is limited, you can say you're running out, even if it's not urgent at that moment.

If people aren't stopping, you may need to reach out to people and...

...Engage physically.

Any type of physical engagement will make the person more invested in your conversation. If you know some of the basic rules of dating and body language, you know that "touch" is a very positive point of engagement.

"Touch" can refer to human contact, such as a handshake. It also can refer to two people holding an object together, or simply the moment you hand the object over to the other person.

If you are handing over an object, don't let go right away. Keep holding for a moment longer. It's unlike handing out a flyer where the recipient takes it, walks away, and then throws it into the nearest receptacle. The momentary "hold" during the handover will be slightly awkward, but now you've got the "mark" invested and you can easily mirror their actions as you're talking about the object. Very few people will hand the object back to you once they've accepted.

The object acts as a mutual touchpoint. If someone is holding an object, such as a document or an iPad®, it's an anchor. They're locked in one location, thus allowing you to point things out with their now undivided attention. Having a participant hold and look at an object with you is a common technique magicians use to keep a person's focus in the right place.

To get someone to grab the object, hand it to them and say...

..."Here's something amazing."

It's a great opening line, but it requires a payoff. Many marketers and salespeople will say their product is amazing, but can they back it up? If you can announce something is amazing and then show it to the person that very moment, they'll never forget you.

If you don't have something amazing to show off, you can simply just say "Hello," the person's name, and then...

...Qualify the person quickly.

We can all talk, and if you wanted to you could chat up one entertaining person for hours. But that's not an ideal goal at a trade show. Not everyone is right for your company and your product. And even if they are, there are more people you need to meet. Qualify a person quickly to save both you and them time at the trade show.

After your open-ended question, move into a question for which the answer will pre-qualify them (allowing you to hand them off to someone), collect their information, engage in further dialogue, or end the conversation.

Standard qualifying questions could be:

- Are you responsible for buying at your company?

- Are you having a problem with *X*?

- Are you here looking for and reviewing solutions for your company?

These questions may only identify a single type of person. If you have a very complicated product, or you're trying to sell to enterprises...

...Have different qualifiers for different decision makers.

A question that might qualify one person might disqualify another. For example, you wouldn't ask an open-ended sales question to a technical person. They probably won't know the company's annual sales. But the only way you can find out is to ask.

Unlike in dating, you don't have to tiptoe around critical issues such as "Do you want kids?" On a trade show floor, you can be direct and just ask the person:

- Are you looking for a solution to *X*?

- What is your role within the company?

- Are you evaluating or authorizing purchases?

- Do you know how much volume your company is handling?

- What's your role within the organization?

Obviously you don't want to make those your opening lines, but it's perfectly okay to ask the questions straight up. Problem is, it's not that memorable. Your best bet is to...

...Add a gimmick to your question.

Whether people qualify or not, you don't want anyone to forget you and your company. To be unforgettable, either have a fantastic story that sticks (read Chip and Dan Heath's book *Made to Stick*) and/or come up with a fun attention-grabber that requires people to engage and remember you.

For Live Marketing's client ACI Worldwide, a payments software client, the event production company came up with a gimmick for passersby at a banking show. ACI Worldwide had two goals at the conference: to identify people who were concerned with check fraud, and to further identify those who thought it was at least a $500 million problem.

Booth exhibitors would stop a passerby, show them a check, and ask them: "Excuse me, do you think this check is forged?" This gimmick gave the exhibitor an excuse to stop an attendee and engage them in a conversation about check fraud, ultimately asking the attendee if they thought check fraud was at least a $500 million problem.

If they didn't think it was a $500 million problem...

...The prospect is not qualified. End the conversation gracefully.

You want to be friendly to everyone you meet, but not everyone you meet is going to be right for your company. You really can't waste time with an unqualified prospect. And an unqualified prospect doesn't want to waste their time with you, either. Politely end your conversation quickly, without making the person feel like you're blowing them off. Even if this person is not a prospect, you still want to project a positive brand to the rest of the industry.

To end the conversation gracefully, do the following:

REPEAT YOUR COMPANY'S NAME AND STORY: Spend an extra 20 seconds to make sure the person remembers your company's name and what you do.

PREPARE CLOSING LINES: Just like you prepared opening lines, you should also prepare a few closing lines. Trade show presenter Richard Laible's favorite closing line is "Great to meet you. Have a great show." When you offer up a closing line, make direct eye contact, shake their hand, and be sincere. Without it, you will have just destroyed what might have been a good yet unqualified engagement.

"You want everyone to have a good experience and know what you do whether they're qualified or not," said Matt Hill. Every person you meet has a network of their own. And chances are pretty high they'll know someone who is qualified. If you did a good job explaining your company's story so they remember it, then they'll be able to retell it to someone else, possibly to people at the conference.

In the ACI Worldwide case, if the prospect thought check fraud *was* a $500 million problem then...

...The prospect is qualified. In most cases you'll still need to end your conversation quickly.

You know you have to disengage with an unqualified prospect, but you also have to do the same with a qualified prospect. If someone is interested in your company, you'll feel compelled to talk with them at great length. It'll be desirable and a comfortable feeling especially if you've undergone a lot of rejection and/or unqualified prospects. But that's not your job. Your job is to connect with as many qualified prospects as possible.

It's a lot easier to find one qualified person that wants to talk for 20 minutes than 10 qualified people that want to talk for two minutes each. Instead of going the route of least resistance, you must take the more difficult path.

At a trade show, time is not on your side. Try to fight the urge to gab to just one person. While you want to maintain focus with that one person when you're talking with them, be aware that the benefit of being at a trade show is that it's a room filled with industry people. All of them are literally within arm's reach and could turn into seven-figure customers. While you may be talking to a great prospect, there are lots of other great prospects out there as well. Collect as many as you can.

Trade shows are *not* for closing deals. "You're there to meet them, engage them, and follow up with them later," explained Richard Laible.

When you do find a qualified prospect, begin setting the foundation for the relationship. Make your meeting meaningful and memorable, and make it stick. If you want that person to remember you and your company...

...Engage them in *your story.*

How do you do what you do? What's an amazing case study that really shows off your capability? Tell a quick anecdote or case study that really demonstrates your company's capabilities. Previously, we suggested you have three stories in the can. Those stories could be about your company or a story about the industry. If you want them to buy from you, ultimately you're going to have to tell your story.

Part of telling your story is to truly engage them in your tale. Constantly look to them and ask questions that require either agreement or for them to fill in the blanks of your story. For example, a dialogue could go something like this:

"We had a client that had a situation like _____. Are you facing a similar problem?"

"They had previously used _____ [a competitor's product]. Have you ever used that product, or something similar?"

"Upper management was requiring that they show some proof of success. Have you felt similar pressure?"

While you're engrossed in conversation, still keep one eye on the rest of the booth, and...

...Don't let attendees stand unapproached.

This is the most common mistake made by exhibitors. It's your booth, yet you let people walk in and out without ever introducing yourself. You wouldn't let someone walk into your home without saying "Hello," so don't do it with your booth.

According to the Center for Exhibition Industry Research (CEIR), if a person with a high level of authority walks into your booth, they'll wait only 15 seconds for someone to approach them before they give up and just walk away. No one would want to blow such a golden opportunity, yet it happens all the time.

Many people use the excuses of "Our booth was really busy" or "If I knew it was *so and so* in our booth... ." If you truly think your booth is going to be that busy, then it's worth it for you to bring in an additional person or people to solely look out for and approach ungreeted people who have entered your booth.

While you may assign one "lookout" to work your booth, everyone must...

...Acknowledge someone is there if they walk up to your conversation.

At a trade show, strangers will walk up to you all the time. And sometimes they'll walk up to you while you're in the middle of a conversation with someone else. They'll stand there politely and wait for you to finish. But if you don't within the first 15 seconds acknowledge the person standing there, they'll walk away and worse, they'll be insulted and they'll probably let someone else know about it.

When you notice someone walk up, either say "I'm going to wrap this up in one minute and then I'll be with you," or much better than that...

...Bring others into your conversation.

How often do you walk into a new restaurant that has no customers? Unless you're desperate you walk over to the next restaurant that has people in it. People attract other people, especially in conversation. You want to make your booth and your conversation look like a popular restaurant.

It's far easier to bring in a second, third, or more person into a conversation than it is to just attract one. When you're alone you look like that empty restaurant.

After you've stopped one person and you're engaged them in conversation, always have one eye out for other people who may slow down or catch your eye as you're talking.

If you do catch someone else's eye, say "Hello" and then a single line about what you're talking about: "Are you interested in..." Then ask the person you're talking with if it's okay if you bring your new friend into the conversation. Introduce the new person to the group.

As people join the group, it's inevitable that a few will leave so...

...Respond to those who walk away.

If you were fortunate enough to assemble a small crowd, expect a few people to leave. Don't take it personally. A trade show floor is filled with distractions and people eventually trail off. If you notice, chances are others will as well and they'll become distracted.

"Did he just notice that guy walking away?"

In almost all cases, you should acknowledge what just happened. If not, your audience may still obsess over the person who just walked away. Ignoring it is usually not a good option.

You have two options here:

OPTION 1: Be honest.

- "Bummer for them, I was just about to get to the best part."

OPTION 2: Make a joke.

- "Another satisfied customer that doesn't need to hear anymore."

- "His company will regret that decision."

- "At least the good-looking/smart people are staying."

- (If they are on the phone) "Ah, looks like he's calling to make his first order."

To keep those who stayed engaged, you could use the previously mentioned technique of endowing. Or if it's in your nature, be silly and...

...Use nicknames as coding for qualified prospects.

Earlier I spoke about endowing people with positive branding. Not only will it endear people to you, but you can also use it to improve the likelihood and process of "holding court" with a small crowd. In addition, it can be used as a type of code to signal those who are the most qualified prospects.

"OK, we've got quite a group here. We've got the David, the smart buyer. Susan, the savvy analyst. And we've got Katherine, the no-nonsense administrator."

Amassing crowds, endowing them, and handing them off to another person is not for rookies. The technique requires honed moderation skills where you can bounce in and out of conversations and keep people engaged. Holding court over a growing conversation takes some finesse and skill.

If you can't do it yourself...

...Hire a magician.

Unlike a standard presenter or other entertainer, a magician skilled at working trade shows knows how to work with crowds, can converse, and his/her work requires attention and focus from the audience. There's no way to enjoy a magician if you're in a conversation or looking at your cell phone. The magician will even instruct people to put their cell phones down because they're not going to want to miss a moment of his/her performance.

In their performance, the magician can ask all the qualifying questions you want and can identify those key prospects for you. With each performance the magician is holding court and locating those best candidates. And by amassing more crowds, they drive more scans and therefore more leads.

While the magician is highly skilled, you can't rely on that one person to do all the engaging for you. Don't expect to learn all of this overnight — you must...

...Practice, practice, practice.

Reading this book will give you a lot of ideas as to what you should do, but it won't be until you actually apply them in a real-world situation that they will actually become effective. There's no conceivable way you can just read this book and assume you're going to both remember and be able to apply everything you learned when you hit the trade show floor.

As much as you may not want to, you absolutely must practice. This is probably the one tip most readers will want to avoid, because they'll think it's a waste of time. "Heck, I know how to talk to people." Yes you do, but you don't necessarily know how to do it in a rapid-fire format where you're constantly making relationships, qualifying people, and moving them through your booth so you can get to the next person.

Remind yourself how much money you're investing at this trade show. You have absolutely no problem shelling out *thousands* to have a booth and for your employees to attend this conference. Are you also calculating all the lost productivity and opportunity cost of your colleagues traveling and not being at work? Why would you gamble on something you're spending so much money on? What other parts of your business do you spend thousands on and then don't prepare?

If you don't do this with other aspects of your business, then don't gamble here. You absolutely must practice.

It doesn't have to be a painful experience. In fact, you can make it a lot of fun with a little experimental...

...Role play.

Want to know how you'd behave trying to stop a big fish? What about someone challenging you with endless questions about your competitors? Or maybe someone who is talking a mile over your head?

Do you have good answers to difficult questions? Have you actually said them out loud and heard another person's reaction?

Even if you've worked trade shows before, your business and industry is constantly changing. You have to be prepared for all the new questions and issues people have.

You want to be able to engage with the most difficult people and still earn their trust. Can you convert a detractor and make them an advocate?

Once again, most people don't feel comfortable rehearsing how they'd behave in a certain environment or playing someone other than themselves, especially in front of their colleagues. That's something usually reserved for private family or couples' therapy. For trade show training...

...Hire an improv coach.

Getting you prepared for a show requires someone who is extremely comfortable teaching unscripted performance. This is where an improv coach could come in really handy. The improv coach will orchestrate a lot of things for you that you've simply had no experience doing, like role playing your new trade show behavior.

While the improv coach will be able to help guide your interaction and behavior, you need to guide him/her so...

...Write down potential customers' top issues.

An improv coach will help you loosen up and practice how to engage with people. What s/he will not know will be the ins and outs of your business. Before the improv coach begins your training, take some time to write down your customers' top issues and how they map to your product's top features and qualities. That way you'll give the improv instructor the ammunition to train your team appropriately for your audience.

One aspect of improv you won't want to mimic is mime. Instead...

...Use actual objects in your rehearsal.

True improv work requires actors to do something known as "object work," which means they mime the aspects of space and behavior of objects and our interactions with them. When you're at a trade show, you're actually interacting with these physical objects. And these objects can break and be cumbersome and get in our way. Make sure you know how to use these objects:

- When you're at the demo station, can you operate the controls while still having a conversation with the person, or is your back to them?

- Have you determined where everyone will be standing and facing?

- How do you collect the information from the person? Are you using a badge scanner? Is it easy to access or do you have to turn your back to the person to get it? Depending on what you do, that small but subtle movement can maintain or alter the relationship just before you gather very sensitive information.

Practice, role play, work with actual objects, and...

...Allow yourself to make mistakes.

Did you ever learn how to drive in the snow and ice? When you start skidding on ice, you're supposed to turn in the direction of the skid. It's not an intuitive thing to do, but it's the right thing to do. If you turn away from the skid, the car will spin out of control. To prepare yourself for that challenge, go to an icy parking lot and try to make your car skid so you can actually feel what it's like to turn into the skid, which is the correct reaction. The purpose is to experience the rough condition in a safe environment before you actually hit the rough condition in a real environment. You're trying to create similar situations with challenging role play.

The harder you try to throw your colleagues off, the more prepared they'll be on the trade show floor. In fact, try to create extremely severe situations. To prepare your colleagues for the worst, think of the most difficult scenarios. When you're extremely well prepared, the actual trade show experience will be far easier.

Look at the Presidential candidates. They rehearse, rehearse, and rehearse for their stump speeches and their debates. They leave very little up to chance.

Here are some fun ways you can role play:

- Have one colleague come to your booth just to tell you how awesome your main competitor is.

- Let one of your colleagues be an annoying attendee, with questions for which you don't know the answer. Let them try to fluster you, and try to keep your cool. Make it a challenge. See who wins.

- Make one of your colleagues monopolize your time while you're trying to get to more qualified attendees.

Whatever challenge is thrown your way...

...Always make direct eye contact.

This is just a good 'ole fashioned networking technique. By focusing and making direct eye contact, you can make a true personal connection. You want that person to walk away with a good experience from you and the brand. Many people have a hard time with this because they get a little self-conscious. You need to get over it. Begin by practicing with people who will know you're doing it. Then start doing it more often when you're networking with people in general. For great politicians, it's second nature.

Whatever you choose to do, your focus has to be on creating a positive, memorable experience. Then you can...

...Scan badges, but only after you've engaged.

Badge scanning can be done in subtle and not-so-subtle ways. I've had experiences where I've walked into a booth and my first contact was with a "booth babe," who immediately held out her scanner and asked to scan my badge. Obviously she'd been instructed by the company to do just that. The problem with such a technique is the experience with the brand is nonexistent. And it's questionable whether it reflects positively or negatively on your brand.

Badge scanning is a type of commerce exchange. I understand my personal information has intrinsic value. You simply can't ask to scan a badge before you've offered something, such as more information or a chance to win a prize, and I've agreed that I'm willing to exchange my personal information for that.

To scan a badge without offering something in exchange is equivalent to saying "Give me a buck." Being a beggar is a brand image you don't want to portray. If you want to scan someone's badge, you absolutely must make the value exchange extremely clear.

To make the experience less awkward, make it appear as part of a normal exchange like you would handing over a business card or money to get a service in return.

"While we're waiting to get your T-shirt, let me scan your badge."

"Let me scan your badge and I'll make sure we forward that information."

Practice how you can physically do the scan so it comes off as a natural interaction. Being "scanned" is not a natural way to engage. It's your job to make it feel natural.

As great as scanning is to collect attendee information...

...Don't rely too heavily on the badge scanner.

Badge scanners are wonderfully efficient tools, and they look high-tech, but they're horrible at building relationships with potential customers. The actual act of using the badge scanner splits your focus and takes you out of the one-on-one engagement state.

While the information from badge scanners may be dumped into your company's Customer Relationship Management (CRM) system, the information scanned will tell you nothing about the relationship you built at that moment.

You can use the badge scanner to input the information, but right after you scan...

...Write some notes about your conversation.

Take a minute to jot down some notes about your conversation. Write it on the back of the person's business card, in your phone, or on a pad of paper. After the event, make sure to input that information into the CRM system. It's better that you, the author of the note, do it, as you'll remember the conversation and be able to add more background information. The note is there just to jog your memory about the conversation.

Taking that extra effort to write notes allows the follow-up to be a continuation of the conversation. Without it, that conversation will be lost forever and you'll be starting from square one. Often "square one" is just a mass-mailed "Thanks for stopping by our booth" follow-up email. Any personal engagement you had with that person is now lost. They would just be a name in a database. If you do capture a few notes and enter it alongside the information captured by the badge scanner, you'll be able to address the person's specific needs.

People are horrible about following up. You've probably handed out hundreds if not thousands of business cards. Have you received hundreds and thousands of follow-up emails and phone calls? To increase your odds of a response...

...Personalize the takeaway.

As you're writing notes down on *their* business card, write some notes down on *your* business card as well. In essence, you're doing for them what you're doing for yourself. Those personalized notes, which could be identifying what your solution is, or something specific to your conversation, will increase the chances they'll follow up with you.

After you've exchanged information, know what the qualified prospect's specific needs are and...

...Close with an action step that furthers the relationship.

Your goal is to lay the foundation of a relationship that could one day turn into business. Trade show booths are rarely designed to close sales. Instead, close your conversation with an action on your part to further the relationship. While the generic action step would be to set up a demo or forward some additional materials, aim for a customized action step that acknowledges you were really *listening*. Here are some examples:

"Let me put you in contact with a customer just like you that had some of the same issues you're having. I think you could really benefit by learning from their experiences."

"We just did an ROI cost analysis for a business very similar to yours. I'll forward those numbers to you. Please feel free to share with your CFO."

"I've written down all your questions that I couldn't answer, and I know just the woman in the office who can answer them. I'll have her respond to your questions."

"I'd love to have you test out our product to see if it works in your environment. I'll have one of my colleagues follow up with you."

When it's time to say goodbye...

...Reward the person for stopping.

Whether you're with a qualified lead or not, a reward is a great positive way to end a conversation. Give the attendee a prize, enter them into a contest, or do something silly and fun like take a photo of them against a superimposed image of the Oval Office (or maybe something relevant to your business).

In the ACI Worldwide case, after the exhibitor showed the attendee the potentially forged check and qualified the person, they were directed to another table to cash the check for a $10 Starbucks card.

If you want to reward unqualified people, you can enter them into a sweepstakes, or it's perfectly OK as mentioned before to politely end the conversation and say goodbye.

From beginning to end, your engagement must always be out in front, at the same level as everyone else so...

...Don't stand behind a desk.

Many booths have counters that PR reps and booth babes stand behind, making them look like customer service reps ready to answer customer complaints or handle a product return. A desk or counter is a physical and mental barrier. It's not inviting at all. Plus, it divides you from the attendees. I'm this person because I'm over here.

Don't stand behind the counter. Stand in front of it.

Virgin America learned this with ticketing, and often you'll see their staff come out from behind the counter to check in travelers.

While you want to attract people to your booth, your goal is not to just load your booth with warm bodies...

...A busy booth doesn't necessarily translate into a successful booth.

Often you'll hear companies talk about how "busy" their booth was at a trade show. Having people in your booth is a great attractor and it does draw more people, but traffic shouldn't be the only measure of success. If you built your booth just for traffic, e.g. T-shirt giveaways, crazy contests, and booth babes, you won't necessarily draw the crowd that you want.

A carnival barker may draw people in, but ultimately you want your staff to reach out, engage, and qualify.

You don't want to just draw any crowd — you want to draw and manage *your* crowd. If you think you're going to be overwhelmed...

...Manage your booth's crowd in layers.

For a very large booth that requires multiple people to staff, your best bet is to create different layers of defense by allowing only the most qualified people access to the most knowledgeable people in your booth. All situations are different, but here's one suggested model:

- **PERIMETER QUALIFIERS**: Hire unskilled employees or outside trade show staffers to work the perimeter. Their job is to engage and ask the scripted qualifying question.

- **KNOWLEDGEABLE STAFFERS**: Qualified attendees are then directed to a booth where a knowledgeable employee is working.

- **FLOATERS**: PR people will often watch for unattended people who might enter the booth, or answer questions that the perimeter qualifiers can't answer.

- **THE "WHALE"**: Using a check-in/check-out procedure, make sure that one C-level or VP-level person is always in the booth in case a high-level top client or top prospect enters the booth.

This may sound overly complicated, but it really isn't. It can work. You just have to...

...Make sure your staff actually works at the event.

Often staff members who attend trade shows treat it like it's a vacation junket to, say, Las Vegas or San Francisco. They schmooze with each other in the booth and talk about the parties, restaurants, and shows they're going to attend later that night. They don't look at staffing the trade show booth as work. Or they feel the complete opposite and see it as a punishment for having to be there. Working a trade show is very much work. In fact, it's really hard, exhausting, and skilled work.

If you're doing your job right at a trade show, you should be completely wiped out at the end of each day. That's because you're on your feet all day and you're constantly talking to people. As mentioned at the beginning of this book, a trade show is a completely unnatural environment. You're doing what you may do in a normal day but at a very rapid and repetitive clip. You're conducting conversations and meetings at a speed you're normally not accustomed to.

Full-time employees who all of a sudden find themselves working in the company trade show booth often feel like a fish out of water. Their job isn't to operate in this unnatural environment and they may have no real incentive to work hard, which is absolutely necessary at a trade show.

For example...

...Salespeople are not always the best people to work the trade show booth.

Since salespeople are by training great schmoozers (true), they'd be perfect in a trade show environment (not true). Booth work takes them away from more immediate money-making opportunities.

One of the first questions a salesman will ask is "Where are you from?" If that person isn't in their territory, they're of no use to them. Salespeople don't want to waste time gathering leads for other salespeople. That's not their job. They want to use their time to work on the leads they already have. There is little incentive for them to lead gather. In fact, they'll resent the marketing department for forcing them to stand at a trade show booth and lead gather for other salespeople. They'd rather leave the booth to take calls or go drinking with existing customers.

It's not just salespeople, but for many working a trade show booth is seen as a punishment so...

...Don't threaten employees to work.

At one trade show, a colleague overheard a boss say to his employees, "I'm paying $700 per person to have you on the show floor. If you don't like it, there's the door." As outlined at the beginning of this book, that manager was fooling himself into believing it only cost him $700 per person to be at a trade show.

Second, what kind of way is that to get anyone to work a trade show booth? If employees don't want to work the booth, don't make them. Instead...

...Require employees to audition to work the booth.

You can turn what is seen as a "punishment" into a "prize" by requiring employees to audition for the honor of traveling gratis to the event and working in the booth. By turning the effort into a contest, booth work will no longer be viewed as a punishment. More importantly, the audition process will cull the most highly motivated employees allowing you to see who will perform the best at the event.

If you're lucky enough to have a brand for which you have rabid customer advocates, you could hold a contest.

Boxee, a video service, held a contest for customers to win a free trip to Las Vegas to work their booth during CES. To enter, you had to send a video of yourself demoing the service, which is what they would be doing at the conference. Boxee posted their favorite videos on their site, let other customers vote, and then picked the winners to come work for free in their booth in Las Vegas.

Make trade show service a prize, not a chore or a punishment. That way you'll get the right people. Whether or not you choose to turn booth participation into a contest...

...Your employees must be incentivized.

Look at all the people working your trade show booth. Who's working harder, your employees or the staff hired just to work the booth?

While the contracted staff doesn't have a vested interest in the success of your business, they do have a vested interest in getting hired again.

Conversely, if you're an employee working the booth and all you do is stand at your station, answer any questions someone has if they walk up to you, and do literally nothing else, it will appear as if you have done your job competently and you'll keep your job.

If someone you hired outside your company did that, they would never work for you again.

To get the most out of employees at a trade show...

...Incentivize staff beyond their job requirements.

Richard Norby of Live Marketing said that cash incentives can turn a lackluster booth into one that's truly working for the company. The most energized booth he ever saw was when the CEO of a company got up in front of his entire staff just before the trade show floor opened and said that if anyone brought someone over to an executive that was using a competitor's product, that would be $50 cash in their hand right there. If that prospect signed with the company, it was $100 cash in hand.

Employees need motivators. And money works. Remember Matt Hill's client who was spending $35,000 an hour to be on the trade show floor? If all it takes is another $50 or $100 to get your employees to actually close that last three feet and qualify connections, wouldn't you do it?

You *have* to incentivize your staff to ensure a return on your investment. Staffers don't need a large extra motivator. A small performance-based cash offering beyond their existing salary can often give them the extra push they need to perform. Fifty dollars for a quality lead is most definitely a comical fraction of what you're spending at the show.

While cash is always a good motivator, you should also...

...Measure booth behavior.

Ask your staff to measure their success engaging with attendees. Assign a point system to each achievement and offer a huge prize for those who get the most points.

There are a host of different behaviors you can measure:

- Who collected the most business cards?

- Who spoke to the most customers?

- Who spoke to the most people working with competitors?

- Who qualified the most leads?

- Who conducted the most demos?

- Who made the most introductions to other staff members?

- Who did the most media interviews?

- Who took the most photos?

- Who tweeted the most about the event?

- Who was retweeted the most?

- Who wrote the most blog posts about the event?

- Who got the most CEO or other C-level business cards?

As the trade show continues, publish their success on the company's intranet for everyone within the organization to see. By counting each action, and publishing it internally, you can acknowledge great performance and build healthy creative tension. Traditionally, companies never offer public commendations or recognition for good work done at a trade show.

Success, though, is a group effort — that's why you don't want to isolate performance...

...Let employees compete in teams.

You can be a lot more successful in dating if you have a wingman/ wingwoman. Same is true with booth engagement. If you never try to close a deal alone, you shouldn't try to operate in a trade show booth alone.

Work in teams of at least two, if not more. Let each person act as a wingman for the other. Let them make warm introductions based on qualifying questions (e.g., "You have to meet Dave, he's got the best solution for your problem").

The money and the awards will get employees excited before the event. But to really crank up their performance...

...Double the incentive once you're at the event.

Surprisingly, it's debatable that people are necessarily motivated by financial incentives. In studies published in the book *Drive* by Daniel Pink, he demonstrated that increasing financial incentives did nothing to improve performance.

Given that we're not sure what will motivate people to work harder, don't try to second-guess your employees. Create multiple incentives and then manage them accordingly. Once you're at the event, double that incentive to get your staff really excited. That could be the result of doubling the money, the prize, or the recognition for a job well done.

While everyone may be competing for these internal "most" awards and to get those cash incentives, ultimately you're all on the same team so...

...Share wisdom and experience at the event.

In theater, after a performance, everyone sticks around for the "show notes", or comments from the director about the night's performance. You should do the same for your trade show booth. At the end of the day, after your daylong performance, have everyone stick around for a few minutes longer and discuss what opening lines and engagement techniques did and didn't work. What are the questions you're hearing? Take advantage of everyone else's experiences, adapt accordingly, and you'll see everyone's success pick up dramatically the next day.

While experiential "in the moment" advice is helpful, there's no getting around the fact that standing on your feet and talking all day can be incredibly exhausting so...

...Have people work in shifts.

Not every company can afford this luxury, but if you can, do it.

If your company is big enough and you've got enough people staffing the booth, then you can and should schedule people in shifts to allow them to mentally and physically relax. People can manage working half days in a booth easily. Two people working half days will give you A-game performance for the full day, since full days can wipe a person out, making them barely functional for the next day. Plus, standing on your feet all day can be exhausting. You don't have to suffer because...

...There is a trick to standing on your feet all day.

Stand straight up, buckle your knees a little, lean forward, and you can stand all day.

Also, and it goes without saying, wear comfortable shoes. If you can avoid it, do *not* wear high heels. If you have to wear heels, get low heeled shoes.

If you truly can't stand all day, even using that technique, get a high director's chair or stool so that you're sitting at eye level with the foot traffic in the aisles.

Even if *you* perfect this technique, most haven't. Make sure you...

...Rent good carpet padding.

Everyone will recognize and appreciate it, and subconsciously attendees will want to stay longer in your booth.

To get them to actually enter your booth, you want to remove every single barrier. Eliminate the most common mental and physical threshold and...

...Rent a carpet that's the same color as the aisles.

When carpet colors of the booth and the aisles are identical, a step from the aisle to your booth is a seamless transition. If the carpeting is of a different color, it feels almost as if one has to make a commitment to enter. People will purposely navigate around you. If you have the same color, it seems natural to just walk right in.

This technique may not always be possible since there may be the need to maintain a consistent color scheme and branding in your booth.

Once attendees are in your booth, you want to make it easy for them to identify people at the company...

...Have everyone wear the same outfit.

It doesn't necessarily have to be a company logo shirt. You could have a luau theme and require everyone to wear a Hawaiian "Aloha" shirt. Whatever costumes you decide, the outfits will show that you're all part of a team, or maybe the cast of a show being performed in your booth. Similarly, if everyone wears a company shirt, then it becomes great advertising as they walk around the show floor.

Matching outfits may not be necessary, though. Sometimes you have to...

...Mix up what people wear.

When people are not in costumes but dressed in business professional attire, it also helps people walk into your booth. But on the flip side, you can purposely wear something silly like the aforementioned rabbit ears or a tie that lights up. That outrageous accessory of flair can actually be your opening line and a point of conversation.

Whatever outfit you choose to wear, always be on your best behavior. Present yourself professionally and...

...Don't eat, drink, work on your computer, talk on the phone, or text in the booth.

We eat at our desk at work. We take personal calls in the office all the time. But in a trade show booth you're on display. If you eat, drink, work on your computer, talk on the phone, or text, you come off unprofessional and more importantly, completely unapproachable. Sadly, it's done all the time and people don't think anything of it. As mentioned at the beginning of this book, your non-verbal communications speak the loudest. Simply don't do these things. It looks really bad.

That's how to solve the problem of looking bad. As for *smelling* bad...

...Use mints and deodorant.

Have a full honesty policy in your booth with fellow staffers. If someone smells or their breath stinks, make sure you tell each other about it. At every trade show you always run into one person whose breath stinks. You keep backing away so you're not downstream of their breath and they keep coming towards you. Be proactive and pop a mint a few times throughout the show. Also have some deodorant handy.

How silly would it be if you lost a potential client because of bad breath? It's a problem that could have been solved with a two-cent mint.

If people are walking away from you as you're talking, they're telling you something so...

...Check your body language.

We don't realize it sometimes, but besides bad breath, simple body movements can actually turn people away. For example, folding your arms or standing at the edge of the booth is off-putting. As Richard Laible explained, you actually want to stand three feet back from the booth's edge and have the attendee walk to the edge of the booth. If you get them to take a step into the booth, you've actually pre-qualified them. Once they're in, you want to...

...Read your target's body language.

If they're incorporating touch, you should consider incorporating touch. If they create a physical space between you, lean in a little to see if they're welcoming. If they fold their arms, force them to open up by getting them to hold something for you. If they look standoffish or reserved, see if you can break that exterior by changing the situation. If they're overtly friendly, that's an open door for you to do the same. Always use your best judgement as no matter what you do, you need to maintain professionalism.

When it's time for you to take a break...

...Coordinate check-in and check-out.

How often has someone come by your booth asking for a specific person and you simply don't know where they are? The answer is often "Oh, she must have just wandered off. She'll be back soon." The response is usually "OK, I'll come back." And then they rarely do. That's the first step towards a failed relationship.

Create a very visible message board in your booth where people can check-in and check-out, messages can be left, and people can leave notes as to when they'll return. Whenever someone comes by looking for someone, which always happens, just refer to the board. If they're not there, let the prospect leave a message that they know will be received.

When you do step out...

...Use your time wisely when you're not working the booth.

If you're lucky enough to only be working a half day in the booth, take advantage of your away time. Simply learn more about your industry by attending a session, do some competitive intelligence, socialize with a prospect or client over coffee, a drink, or a meal.

When you come back...

...Be prepared to do three jobs.

In a trade show environment, everyone's office roles fall away as each individual's time is at a premium. Everyone pitches in to pick up each other's slack. You'll find yourself demoing products that aren't in your department, or answering questions for which you're not an expert. Simply be prepared to handle other people's work.

More importantly, be a cheerleader and a wingman. If you see a colleague has roped in a great candidate, go in to show some support. "You're talking to Dave? You've got our best. He's our number one guy in security." If your colleague is up on stage giving a presentation, you need to cheer and applaud like mad, even if you've already seen his presentation a dozen times that day.

Always show support for your colleagues and work as a team. It broadcasts a fantastic brand image and people will want to be part of your group.

You want everyone to be able to do multiple jobs so...

...Make sure everyone in the booth is media trained.

Given the intense volume of social media being captured and transmitted, anyone can and will be recorded. Don't leave all your media appearances up to one person who may or may not be in the booth or available.

The most insulting thing that happens at a booth, and it happens all the time, is when I walk up to someone who is demoing a product and a PR person sees my press badge and interrupts me and says, "Oh no, you don't want to talk to that person, you want to talk to our VP (CEO, whatever)." I find that maneuver colossally insulting to both the person I'm talking to and to me. I always say, "That's okay, I'm talking with this person and s/he is doing an excellent job explaining your product to me."

Before we close out, I want to address the question of booth babes. Do me a favor and...

...Stop hiring booth babes. It doesn't work.

Unless you're working in the adult film industry, stop hiring attractive women who have no knowledge of your product to be booth ambassadors. Also known as booth babes, booth bunnies, and a series of other sexist names, it simply doesn't pan out.

Marketer Spencer Chen of Axiom Zen demonstrated the failure of booth babes by conducting a split test at a trade show. One booth had the traditional booth babes and the other booth had booth ambassadors who were actual grandmothers. In his study, he showed that the older women gathered more leads than the booth babes.

This is just one study, but booth babes are simply window dressing who detract from the value of your product. Some attendees will be intimidated by them or they'll actually be turned off by them. Unless these beautiful women are intrinsic to your product (fashion, cosmetics, etc.), don't use them. Instead...

...Hire high-end booth staffers.

The advice in this book requires a lot of training to get right. If you feel it'll be too difficult to train your staff, because of cultural reasons or time constraints, or because changing behavior would be like moving a mountain, then you should consider supplementing or replacing your staff with contractors who already know how to do all of the above really well.

These are people who can be trained to understand your product and/or your new announcement, and engage with the audience. Because they're contractors, they'll have a built-in incentive to perform much better than your own staff. If they don't bring in great leads, they won't get hired again. If your staff doesn't bring in great leads, they"l probably still keep their job. You may want to consider leaving half of your staff at the office and replacing them with high-end booth staffers.

FINAL CONSIDERATIONS

CONCLUSION #1: Changing behavior doesn't happen overnight.

It's great you took the time to read this guide — a wonderful first step — but book learning will never replace let alone surpass experience. I know I mentioned this before (re: "Practice, Practice, Practice."), but I can't stress it enough. Your initial reaction to rehearsing at a trade show booth will be to immediately want to blow it off and declare it's a waste of your time. It's not. It's quite the opposite. The few hours of practice you put in before working a trade show booth will be the most effective time you spend. It's important to get a good coach to walk you through the steps and challenge you.

Changing behavior doesn't happen overnight. Training will definitely help but it needs to be ongoing, as changing and shifting behavior requires a learning curve that takes time. That time, money, and effort you spend is worth it, because at a trade show, you're always "Three Feet from Seven Figures."

CONCLUSION #2: Take responsibility. Don't depend on the conference to deliver results.

While conferences and trade shows vary in quality, you can still get value out of the worst ones, solely because there are people there with similar interests as you. Anytime someone tells you that a conference or trade show sucked, ask them if they met anyone new. If they did, ask them what they learned from that person. If they didn't, then don't send them to any more trade shows.

People who say "This show sucked" are either too shy to talk to anyone and therefore the "show sucking" is their fault; or, they measure the value of a trade show by the number of cool whiz-bang things they see.

Half of the success of a trade show depends on connecting with the attendees. If you're not getting anything out of the trade show, you haven't been applying the correct techniques.

You could TRIPLE your leads with Spark Media Solutions' trade show training

If you like what you've read and want to learn more, then please contact us at Spark Media Solutions for trade show training. We have programs to audition your staff, train them, and then build incentive programs to make sure everyone is working as hard as possible during those few very precious hours during the conference. We can train your staff in your office and in real-time on the trade show floor during your event.

You'll love the results. We've had clients *triple* their expected leads after taking our training.

We all know sponsoring a trade show is an expensive and risky business. Don't take anymore trade show risks. Please contact us at info@sparkmediasolutions.com.

TradeShowTraining.net

About Spark Media Solutions

Spark Media Solutions (SparkMediaSolutions.com) is a brand journalism and media consulting firm, founded in 2007. The San Francisco Bay Area company produces content mostly for trade shows and conferences. The content marketing firm refers to its technique as a PR 180°, or creating media about others. The simple philosophy of paying attention to others through media production optimally and cost-effectively increases search visibility and social sharing, as well as grows industry relations. Similar to how any media outlet can grow its brand and industry recognition through the creation of content, so can any business. Spark Media Solutions' "content is the currency of social media and search" and "influencer relations through content" models have proven to be repeatedly successful since the company's inception.

SPARK MEDIA
SOLUTIONS

BIOS

About the Author – David Spark

David Spark (@dspark) is a veteran tech journalist and founder of Spark Media Solutions (sparkmediasolutions.com), a brand journalism firm that helps its clients be seen as leading voices in their fields through brand-quality media production. The company has worked with clients such as IBM, Oracle, Microsoft, Dice, Yammer, IGT, Sprint, Alcatel-Lucent, Tripwire, Riverbed, Zoho, and IndyCar Racing.

Since 1996, Spark and his articles have appeared in more than 40 media outlets including eWEEK, Wired News, PCWorld, ABC Radio, John C. Dvorak's "Cranky Geeks," KQED's "This Week in Northern California," and TechTV (formerly ZDTV).

In addition to traditional media, Spark spent ten years working in advertising and marketing at various agencies, the last being Publicis Dialog, where as New Media Director he launched the company's New Media division. Spark also squandered more than a dozen years working as a touring standup comedian, a San Francisco tour guide, and comedy writer for The Second City in Chicago.

Today, Spark co-hosts the weekly Tear Down Show podcast on the PodcastOne network, and produces the Content Marketing Tips video series. He blogs at the Spark Minute, and has been a regular contributor for Mashable, Socialmedia.biz, and Technologizer. Spark is a happily married father of two boys and lives in the San Francisco Bay Area.

About the Illustrator – Christina Taylor Brown

Christina Brown (@stinabmarie) is a Southern, self-taught artist who enjoys using whimsy and humor to bring her illustrations to life. She has won numerous awards for her artwork, including recognition and ribbons from the city of Houston, Texas. Christina currently lives in Louisiana with her husband, their son, and mischievous dog and cat. She enjoys painting and fills most of her days with illustrating and care of their home and family. Her work can be found at Christina Taylor Brown Illustrations (CBrownIllustration.com).

About Spark Media Solutions' Lead Trainer – Robert Strong

Robert Strong (@robertstrong) is a trade show magician, and owner of Strong Entertainment (StrongEntertainment.com). Since 1985, Strong has been crisscrossing the world and entertaining crowds, has appeared on every major TV network, and has taken his act to all 50 states, more than 40 different countries, and twice at the White House. He specializes in trade show presenting. He is an expert at gathering crowds, entertaining them, communicating the company's message, capturing the leads for follow-up, qualifying the leads by finding out who makes the buying decisions, and connecting those people to the sales staff. For the past decade, Robert has been focused on providing training workshops for Fortune 500 companies' staff on the essentials for success at trade shows.

Acknowledgment

This book would not have been possible without the wise contributions of the following people:

- Matt Hill, President of The Hill Group

- Richard Laible, Trade Show Presenter

- Mike McAllen, Founder of Grass Shack Events and Media

- Mark Norby, Executive Vice President of Live Marketing

- Richard Norby, Principal at Miles North Productions

- Andy Saks, Founder, Spark Presentations

- Robert Strong, Comedy Magician

- John Wall, Host of the blog and podcast, Marketing Over Coffee

More books and content from David Spark:

80 Annoying Communications That Must End

An Internet-popular five-year compilation of the most annoying ways in which we communicate online and in person.

Available on Kindle and Apple iBook. Only $.99.

bit.ly/80annoying

Hazardous to Your Social Media Health:
50 Previously Condoned Behaviors We No Longer Recommend

Instead of advice of what more you can do, this book gives you advice on what you can stop doing in social media, thereby saving you time. In this book, Spark reaches out to 56 industry experts and asks, "What was once considered good advice regarding social media that you either did, advised, or agreed with, but now, given the rapidly changing social media landscape, you no longer recommend?" This ebook is a compilation of their advice.

Available on Kindle, Apple iBook, and PDF. FREE. Registration to Content Marketing Tips newsletter required.

bit.ly/social_hazard

Tear Down Show

Co-hosts David Spark and Michael Wolf discuss the week's tech and media news.

soundcloud.com/teardownshow

Content Marketing Tips newsletter

Register for the Content Marketing Tips newsletter at Spark Media Solutions.
Fun B2B content marketing news and tips delivered to your inbox.

SparkMediaSolutions.com

Content Marketing Tips video series

Media tips for communications professionals. Subscribe today, and watch videos on social media faux pas, trade show prep, and content creation.

youtube.com/sparkmediasolutions